VICTORIAN AND EDWARDIAN
PERTHSHIRE
FROM RARE PHOTOGRAPHS

VICTORIAN AND EDWARDIAN
PERTHSHIRE
FROM RARE PHOTOGRAPHS

RAYMOND LAMONT-BROWN

AND

PETER ADAMSON

FOREWORD

BY

THE RT. HON. THE EARL OF PERTH, P.C.

ALVIE PUBLICATIONS ST ANDREWS

First published in 1985 by
Alvie Publications
52 Buchanan Gardens
St Andrews KY16 9LX
(Tel: 0334 75227)

ISBN 0 950 6200 92

Printed in Scotland by
Allen Litho
Kirkcaldy

Contents

ACKNOWLEDGEMENTS

The authors wish to express their sincere thanks to the following for their help and enthusiastic support in the compilation and preparation of this book:

The Rt. Hon. the Earl of Perth, P.C., Mr R Smart, Dr D Sinclair, Professor W Stibbs, Dr J Robertson, Mr. W Gardiner, Rev Tom Dick; Mr J Blair, Miss S Payne, Dr R P Doig, Mr D Nimmo, Mr D Gibson, Mr S Campbell, Mrs E Thomson, Mr B Nodes and Mr M Cooper. The authors are most grateful to Dick Caddy of Allen Litho for his enthusiastic help. A special thanks too goes to Mr A C McKerracher F.S.A. Scot. for permission to use extracts from his book *Portrait of Dunblane 1875-1975.*

Photographic credits and sources:

The Rt. Hon. the Earl of Perth P.C., 55, 76, 90, 101, 107, 116, 117, 138, 173.

Sir James Cayzer, Bt., 111, 112, 113, 114, 115.

The Hon. Mrs Cherry Drummond of Megginch, 118, 119, 120.

The Hon. Ronald Eden, 133.

The Rt. Hon. the Earl of Mansfield and Mansfield, 108, 109, 110.

Mr A Chinnery-Haldane, 102, 103.

His Grace the Duke of Atholl, 2, 98, 104, 105, 106, 124, 155, 156.

Mr D Davidson, 10, 30, 31, 33, 34, 36, 81, 93, 135, 140, 148, 151, 166, 168, 169.

Perth Museum and Art Gallery, Frontispiece, 43, 64, 68, 74, 75, 78, 80, 96, 125, 127, 130, 131, 132, 141, 152, 153, 160, 162, 172.

Mr S Summers, 4, 32, 51, 52, 53, 57, 58, 59, 60, 65, 67, 70, 71, 72, 73, 87, 99, 128, 150, 154, 161. 154, 161.

Mr E Stewart, 44, 97, 129.

Miss Elizabeth McIntosh, 5, 6, 14, 37, 39, 54, 86, 88, 100, 145, 158, 163, 164.

Mrs Rhyder, 7.

Mr & Mrs F Neil, 9, 11, 91, 92, 136, 137.

Muthill Museum, 13, 165, 167.

The Library, The University of St Andrews, 15, 41, 48, 50, 51, 56, 61, 62, 83, 149, 157.

Mrs M Simm, 40, 63.

Mrs Mary Forsyth, 159.

Mr D McDonald, 16, 17, 25, 77, 122, 123.

Dundee District Libraries Photographic Collection, 18, 19, 20, 21, 35, 38, 42, 45, 121.

Mrs A Watt, 22, 29.

Mr D Phillips, 23, 24.

Mr J Mitchell, 26, 49, 144.

Mrs A Anton, 27.

Mrs E Mailer, 28, 126.

Mr R Robertson, 66, 84, 85.

Mrs M McDonell, 69.

Mr H Simm, 79, 170.

The Estate of the late Major D Stewart, 82.

The Black Watch Museum, 94, 95.

Mrs D Smith, 12, 146, 147.

Mr Peter and Lady Margaret Stirling-Aird of Kippenross, 8, 47, 171.

Mr L Marshall, 46.

Mrs B Grant, 134.

Mr J. Wright, 89.

The Rt. Hon. Lord Home of the Hirsel K.T., P.C., D.L., 3.

Auld Abernethy Association, 139, 142, 143.

FOREWORD

By The Rt. Hon. the Earl of Perth, P.C.

EVERY STUDENT of early photography knows about the work of Hill and Adamson but there were throughout Scotland in the last half of the 19th century many other skilled photographers whose work is little known—if at all. The Scottish National Portrait Gallery has recently started the Scottish Photography Archive to record their work. Peter Adamson and Raymond Lamont-Brown have independently done a splendid job in tracing and chasing photographs in Perthshire which show its social life and scenery in town and country.

I am happy to write this foreword to this book which records the outcome of their labours. This was especially because my great-grandfather, W. H. Drummond, later 9 th Viscount Strathallan was a pioneer of the art starting in the 1840s. Some of his photographs are to be found in this book and the self-portrait must be one of the very earliest. He appears as a tall, looming figure with a tower of Strathallan Castle as backdrop. He placed the camera on the ground, ran to the chair already exactly placed and focused and there stood very still leaning on it for several minutes. I remember his daughter, Fanny, my great-aunt, telling me what a bore it was (I nearly wrote he was!) having the members of his family pose motionless for quite a while. Perhaps this explains why many of his early portraits are of his staff—they more or less had to do what they were told!

When first approached about this project for this book I was somewhat hesitant—but how wrong I was! What a feast of the social history of Perthshire is spread before us. There are here good old days with picturesque towns and villages, the bustle of carriage and cart, the life of the grand house and the record of traders and individuals whose craft has vanished.

I am sure that all who see this book will enjoy it. If it leads to readers searching their attics for old photographs that will be good; if the finds are reported to their local museums or to the Photography Archive in Edinburgh that will be better, and if the sequel is another book on Perthshire's photographic past that will be best of all.

Perth

Frontispiece
1. A lamplighter repairs the light above the distinctive iron public lavatory at the South St Port, Perth. The lavatory was demolished between the wars as it caused an obstruction to vehicular traffic. The old lady in the foreground is probably the Perth hawker known as 'Blue Caum Kate'. She would receive her nickname from the slate pencil (caum) used to whiten a hearth or doorstep.

VICTORIAN AND EDWARDIAN PERTHSHIRE FROM RARE PHOTOGRAPHS

INTRODUCTION

BEFORE THE DAYS of Queen Victoria, Perth was not a well known metropolis to the average Briton. A milestone in the re-awakening of Perth to its flourishing activities of Victoria's reign was undoubtedly the completion of the Bridge of Perth by the English engineer, John Smeaton (1724-92), in 1772. For approximately a hundred and fifty years goods had been ferried to the town across the Tay and the pace of life was slow. George St and Charlotte St were formed as approaches to the new bridge, and the city, once the ancient capital of Scotland, drew its second breath. The slopes of Kinnoull Hill were to see the development of mansion and villa, and within the town such developments as the County Buildings and Courthouse (1823), with its projecting portico, erected on the site of Gowrie House gardens, was to set the style for new public works. Another development was to be mentioned in one of the very few contemporary descriptions of the period.

Thomas Frognall Dibdin (1776-1847), the English bibliographer, noted this about Perth during his visit in 1837: 'On descending from the heights, the whole town has a fine aspect, reminding me, I know not why, of the smart, cheerful air of a provincial town in England. A broad and noble bridge of stone bestrides the River Tay. To the right is a beautiful racecourse of rich turf, enfiladed by the river, and having to the left some fine street scenery. But what most struck me, on my first approach to Perth—descending from the upper road to Kinfauns Castle [*the home of Francis Gray, 15th Baron Gray, 1765-1842, Postmaster General of Scotland*]— was the Water Works, of which Mr. Professor Anderson had both the construction and direction. Here was a lesson to learn—or a model to copy—for all England. Here was deformity converted into beauty, and a nuisance rendered a picturesque accessory.'

Dibdin, or course, was referring in his mention of the 'Water Works' to The Round House in Marshall Place which became a Victorian showplace. So much so that in 1837, Frederick William III, King of Prussia, obtained a set of plans of the enterprise and ordered a facsimile of the building to be erected in Berlin. Prior to the reign of George IV, Perth obtained its water from town wells, the Town Lade and the River Tay. There were no means of purification in those days and the contaminated water led to many outbreaks of disease. Little more was done after the Town Council ordered the construction of a pump at the foot of the High St in 1751 to develop the water supply until in 1810 Dr Adam Anderson, Rector of Perth Academy (he became Professor of Natural and Experimental Philosophy in the University of St Andrews in 1837; he died in 1846) was appointed to advise the town on its water supply. Time passed, however, and the worsening condition of Perth's water supply caused the Council to act and Professor Anderson's scheme to construct a filter gallery in the River Tay was approved. The Round House was the result as the pumping station and the whole scheme was completed in 1832.

The Victorian Age began at twelve minutes past two on the morning of 20 June 1837, on the death of His Majesty King William IV. He was succeeded by his niece Georgina Charlotte Augusta Alexandrina Victoria, daughter of H.R.H. Prince Edward, Duke of Kent (1767-1820) and his wife Victoria, Princess of Saxe-Coburg (1786-1861).

Queen Victoria visited Perth and Perthshire during her first trip to Scotland, August-September 1842 when she was 25, accompanied by Prince Albert, whom she had married in 1840. In her party too, was her remaining 'wicked uncle' Adolphus, Duke of Cambridge (1774-1850). On Tuesday, 6 September, Victoria and her entourage first entered Perthshire. In her

Leaves From The Journal Of Our Life In The Highlands (1867) Victoria recorded her first impressions:

'We changed horses next at the Bridge of Earn. . . . At half-past three we reached Dupplin, Lord Kinnoull's [*The 10th Earl of Kinnoull (1785-1866), Lord Lieutenant of Perthshire*]. All the time the views of the hills, and dales, and streams were lovely. The last part of the road [*was*] very bad travelling, up and down hill, Dupplin is a very fine modern house with a very pretty view of the hills on one side, and a small waterfall close in front of the house. A battalion of the 42nd Highlanders was drawn up before the house, and the men looked very handsome in their kilts. We each received an address from the nobility and gentry of the country, read by Lord Kinnoull; and from the Provost and Magistrates of Perth. We then lunched. The Willoughbys, Kinnairds, Ruthvens and Lord Mansfield, and one of his sisters, with others, were there. After luncheon, we walked a little way in the grounds, and then at five o'clock we set off again. We very soon came upon Perth, the situation of which is quite lovely; it is on the Tay, with wooded hills skirting it entirely on one side, and hills are seen again in the distance, the river winding beautifully'.

The 'Kinnairds' and 'Ruthvens' mentioned by Victoria, were George William Fox Kinnaird, Lord Kinnaird of Inchture (1807-78), Master of the Queen's Buckhounds, and his wife Francis; and the Scottish peer, James Ruthven of Freeland (1777-1853), and his wife Mary.

The Provost of Perth, mentioned too by Victoria, was Baillie C.G. Sidey, who because of the long absence of sovereigns in Scotland had to consult the Lord Chamberlain's department on protocol. Sidey was particularly anxious to know on which side of the carriage the Queen should sit, which knee was to be bent, the position of his carriage in the procession, and when to put on his *Chapeau de bras* (his three-cornered hat). The Provost presented the keys of the city to Victoria and Albert was made a Freeman. A Triumphal Arch, the work of Patrick Wallace, was set up in Atholl St. Thereafter the royal party went to Scone, then the home of William David (1806-98), the 4th Earl of Mansfield.

Queen Victoria left Scone next day and travelled north to Dunkeld where she lunched and watched highland dancing, thence on to Taymouth, the granite castle of the 2nd Marquess and 5th Earl of Breadalbane (1796-1862). The company stayed two days to shoot on the Breadalbane estates, while Victoria walked and drove around the neighbourhood. Visits were made to Glen Dochart, Lochearnhead, Comrie and by 11 September, Victoria had arrived at Drummond Castle to be the guest of the 19th Baron Willoughby de Eresby (1782-1865). Albert went forth once more to kill the local fauna. On 13 September, Victoria was travelling again from Drummond Castle, via Ardoch and Greenloaning to Dunblane and thence left the county. By this time the Queen's entourage had swelled to 656 horses.

Victoria returned to Perthshire in September 1844 on an official visit to Blair Atholl. Again she was accompanied by Prince Albert, and was joined by the 3rd Earl of Liverpool, Lord Steward of her Household, the 4th Earl of Aberdeen (1784-1860), her Foreign Secretary, and Sir James Clark, Physician to the Queen. This time the Queen's oldest child, Victoria, the Princess Royal, was of the party.

At Coupar Angus the party entered Perthshire. In her *Journal* Victoria wrote the following, which gives an excellent picture of what the Victorian tourist would see: 'The harvest is only now being got in, but is very good; and everything much greener than in England. Nothing could be quieter than our journey, and the scenery is so beautiful! It is very different from England: all the houses built of stone; the people so different,—sandy hair, high cheek-bones; children with long shaggy hair and bare legs and feet; little boys in kilts. Near Dunkeld, and also as you get more into the Highlands, there are prettier faces. Those jackets which the girls wear are so

2. Queen Victoria and her faithful gillie, John Brown. The queen was eminently photogenic, and she took to the new invention with great enthusiasm. If the camera recorded the plumpness of her figure and the severeness of her expression it also recorded the resoluteness of her character. The queen was born on 24 May 1819 at Kensington Palace and reigned longer than any other British monarch. While she was sovereign, 1837-1901, Britain became the most powerful empire ever known. Victoria was the first monarch ever to be photographed and she particularly liked prints which underlined the virtues of domesticity and family life.

pretty; all the men and women, as well as the children, look very healthy.'

'. . . We crossed the River Isla, which made me think of my poor little dog "Isla". For about five or six miles we went along a very pretty but rough crossroad, with the Grampians in the distance. We saw Birnam Wood and Sir W. Stewart's [*Sir William Drummond-Stewart's (1796-1871) house 'Rohallion'*] place in the fine valley on the opposite side of the river. All along such splendid scenery, and Albert enjoyed it so much—rejoicing in the beauties of nature, the sight of mountains, and the pure air.'

'The peeps of Dunkeld, with the river Tay deep in the bottom, and the view of the bridge and cathedral, surrounded by the high wooded hills, as you approach it, were lovely in the extreme. We got out at an inn (which was small, but very clean) at Dunkeld, and stopped to let Vicky have some broth. Such a charming view from the window! Vicky stood and bowed to the people out of the window.'

On leaving Dunkeld, the royal party was joined by Lord Glenlyon, and paused at Logierait to partake of 'Athole brose' (composed of honey, whisky and milk) thence travelled to Blair Atholl. Lord Glenlyon was George Augustus Frederick John Murray, 2nd Baron Glenlyon, 6th Duke of Atholl (1814-64), who had married Anne Home-Drummond of Blair Drummond (1814-97), Mistress of the Robes to Queen Victoria.

Victoria remained at Blair Castle until 1 October spending her time walking, driving around the beauty spots from Tilt to Bruar, observing ptarmigan, plovers, grouse and pheasants and learning about the history of the area. Victoria visited Blair again during her 'Third Great Expedition' of 1861, and passed by it on her trip to Inverlochy in 1873. The furniture used by Queen Victoria and Prince Albert during the visit of 1844 is still to be seen in the Banvie Room at Blair Castle.

During her visit to Glasgow in 1849 Victoria made a sojourn in Perth. The royal party stayed at the George Inn where they had rested on Friday, 29 September 1848. It is interesting to note that, owing to a sudden change of plan that day, Victoria arrived at the George Inn after only two hours' notice. Yet she received such excellent service and was so pleased with the accommodation provided, that she declared the hotel to be the 'Royal George Inn'. A visit was made to Moncrieffe estate (then the home of Sir Thomas Moncrieffe; the house was destroyed by fire in 1957). While in Perth, Prince Albert took the opportunity of visiting Perth prison.

A prisoner-of-war depot had been built at Perth during 1810-12 by Robert Reid, and this formed the nucleus of the later general prison. A substantial part of that depot still stands and it was used to house prisoners of the Napoleonic Wars of 1789-1815. Following the Act of 1839 additions were made by Thomas Brown in 1839-42, and Robert Matheson in 1852-57. Herein were placed prisoners with sentences of nine months and upwards who were brought from all over Scotland by stagecoach. The prison also housed junior offenders and a few insane prisoners; female convicts were housed here too, after 1885. Perth prison remains the oldest in Scotland.

On her visit to the Invertrossachs in 1869, Victoria again passed through Perth and had a brief halt at Dunblane to view the cathedral; and thence to Callander to the house of Mr (& Lady Emily) Macnaughten, to be hosted by the Macnaughten's niece and nephew, Sir Malcolm and Lady Helen MacGregor. This visit took in the Rob Roy country. When she visited Inveraray in 1875, Victoria rested at Perth for a short while.

Victoria was not the only royal visitor to Perth. In 1847 the town fêted the Grand Duke Constantine (1827-92), the second son of Czar Nicholas I of Russia.

When Queen Victoria came to the throne there were still two Scotlands: the division being the age-old one between Highlands and Lowlands. When she died the division was East and West. Politically Perth and Perthshire reflected the tone of the country and was Liberal Radical. William Ewart Gladstone's approach to the problems of the day was calculated to make a special appeal to the Scot and went down well in Perth and Perthshire. From 1707 to the Reform Act, 1832, Perth was combined with St Andrews, Forfar, Cupar and Dundee to share one Member of Parliament. After the passing of the 1832 Act there were two Members, one for Perth and one for Perthshire. This continued until the new parliament of Gladstone's third term of office in 1886 when Perthshire was divided into East and West as constituencies.

It is interesting to note that, during the election of 24 November 1886, W.E. Gladstone visited Perth (he didn't leave the station). In the welcoming crowd was the Prince of Wales, who later became Edward VII.

Perth was Liberal until 1892 when William Whitelaw of Huntingtower House won the city for the Conservatives. The MPs for Perthshire were predominantly Conservative during 1837-1910.

Behind the average Perthshire man's attitude to politics lay his religion. Default of any kind was incompatible with Calvinist godliness and respectability meant Presbyterianism. Perth was strongly Presbyterian and adhered to the 'Church of Scotland'. As elsewhere in Scotland, prior to 1843, the Perth folk within the Church of Scotland divided into two warring parties: the Evangelicals and the Moderates. The Evangelicals stood for missionary work at home and abroad, and a zealous puritanism that drained Sunday of all pleasure and humour. They attested too, that the congregation of each church had the right to veto the appointment of a minister they disliked and rankled at the suggestion of an appointment of a nominee by a patron. In 1847 most of the Evangelicals had joined the United Presbyterian (U.P.) Church. The Moderates agreed

12

3. H.R.H. Albert Edward, Prince of Wales, around his twenty-first birthday in 1862. As Prince of Wales, Edward had been prevented by his mother from taking any active part in the government of the country, so he had thrown himself enthusiastically into being the leader of a fashionable and idle set whose behaviour scandalised much of contemporary opinion. Even so, Edward was to make the most colourful monarch of modern times although he did not come to the throne until he was sixty.

with patronage and had a much looser rein when it came to dogma and personal behaviour. To them a smile on Sunday and listening to music on the sabbath did not accelerate you to perdition as the Evangelicals averred. Most Moderate ministers rather liked to have recreation, culture and alcohol. By the early 1830s the Evangelicals had had the upper hand at the General Assembly which formed the basis of conflict between the two church parties and in 1843 the less progressive Evangelicals within the Church of Scotland withdrew to form the Free Church of Scotland. By and large the Perth middle class favoured the Free Church. Theology and other disruptions were running battles in the Church of Scotland, and such groupings as the Free Presbyterian Church of 1893 evolved. By 1900 the United Free Church was formed from the Free Church and the United Presbyterian congregations.

Throughout Victorian and Edwardian times in Perth and Perthshire the ministers held a great influence over their flocks. Writing in his book *Doctor's Progress,* R. McNair Wilson had this to say about ministers:

'Ministers formed a class all by themselves, and were a constant source of interest and discussion. Everybody sat "under" one or other of them, and it was a point of honour to uphold your choice as the finest preacher in the country. The sermons were long and usually, insufferably tedious. So much so, indeed, that the jokes fired off at church social gatherings were often, in reality, backhanders at the minister.'

The influence of the Perthshire ministers stemmed from the fact that they were vital link-men between those who had much to give and the needy, for, during 1837-1910, the ministers were very much custodians of the public conscience and were simultaneously interpreters of theology, parish guardians, social welfare officers, burial board governors and educationalists. The responsibilities were great and all ministers had to walk the straight and narrow. One Perth doughty Presbyterian rebuked her minister for taking a walk on a Sunday afternoon.

'But,' said the minister, 'we read that Our Lord Himself walked in the cornfields on the

Sabbath Day.'

The parishioner nodded: 'Aye we do. And I never thought the more of Him for it.'

By and large the Presbyterians of Perthshire had two 'diets' of religion on a Sunday, the services including two lengthy sermons and two 'exposeetions' of Old Testament history. Between the morning and afternoon services the congregations retired to consume 'baps and tea' (or, beer if the wife and the 'meenister wisna' lookin' ').

Throughout Victoria's and Edward's reigns, the Presbyterian churches predominated in Perthshire. Within Perth the Baptists worshipped in South St, then in Tay St (in a building which was originally the Opera House), and the Methodists, who have had a congregation in Perth since 1770, worshipped in Meal Vennel, then the chapel in South St.

Congregationalism in Perth started in the late 18th century. By 1851 a new Congregational Church was established in Canal Crescent, being made up of the members of the old Mill St (1824) congregation. The devotees of the Home Mission Committee of the Evangelical Union applied their efforts to forming their own 'preaching station' in Perth and in 1856, their Perth E.U. Church was established. This church combined with the Mill St congregation to form the church in Kinnoull St, in 1899. Congregational churches were established at Aberfeldy in 1800 and Crieff in 1869.

Generally speaking the folk of Perthshire considered Roman Catholics to be 'beyond the pale' and Episcopalians (the 'Piskies') were held in the greatest suspicion. Many a Presbyterian child skipped down the street chanting: 'Hisky Pisky Amen, Doon on yir knees and up again.' In the more strict households, no hot meals were prepared on a Sunday and therefore, the sight of a 'reekin' lum' in Perthshire meant that the household were 'Piskies'.

Through the Education (Scotland) Act of 1872, the state, for the first time, accepted directly the responsibility of educating children. Even so, the unit of administration remained the parish, burgh, or city, and in the case of Perth, ratepayers were enjoined to elect a school board of between five and fifteen members. The Act required the school boards to enforce attendance, as far as possible, and to appoint teachers, pay their salaries and levy a local rate for education, and fix the amount of school fees that children should pay. At first the charge was around 3d (1p) per week, but after the Act of 1890, elementary education became virtually 'free' in Perthshire; fees continued to be charged for secondary education. Wider powers were given to Perthshire school boards in 1908 when another Education (Scotland) Act was passed. Now the boards had a hand in regular medical examinations and supervision of health in schools, and education for the 5-14 year olds was compulsory.

The evolution of rural education in Perthshire is interesting and one example of this development may be cited from the ancient parish of Madderty. Teaching had begun in the area under the auspices of the Augustinian priory, thence abbey (1220), and continued in one form or another until the responsibility was given into the temporal lordship of William Drummond (later Viscount Strathallan) in 1669. After a lapse during the Reformation, organised teaching began again in the parish and there were schools at Bellyclone and Ardbennie. In the early 1800s a school was set up by Lady Baird of Ferntower, at the village of St David's, to teach girls sewing and needlework. Madderty parish school was opened in 1874 (modernised 1929). Village schoolmasters seemed to spend many years in one place and exercised great influence over the community. At Madderty, Dominie Dunbar (1830-78) was such an influence, and, in 1853, it is recorded his salary was increased to £34.4s.4½d (£34.21) per annum!

There was a Grammar School in Perth in the 12th century, and an Academy for Literature and the Sciences from 1760. In 1807 the Perth Seminaries were established in Rose Terrace to incorporate the Grammar School, the Academy, the English School, the French School, the

Drawing and Painting School and the Writing School. From the 16th century Perth education had been cited for its quality, but it is interesting to note in the Report of the Education Commission (Scotland) of 1868 that the local council were parsimonious in their grants for prizes, teachers' remuneration and the furnishing of classrooms. From the beginning of Victoria's reign the Perth Town Council was responsible for the drawing up of rules as to hours of teaching and subject regulation, but the management of the schools in Perth and Perthshire was transferred to a School Board by the Education Act of 1872.

Up to that Act the designation 'Seminaries' was given to a collection of separate schools in Perth. Thereafter the name Perth Academy was used and the first prospectus was drawn up in 1873. The subjects taught ranged from Classics to Book-keeping and education for girls was fully established. Each subject was charged separately, from Mathematics at 10/6d (52½p) per quarter for one hour daily, to Drawing and Painting at 12/6d (62½p) per quarter for one hour.

Within Perthshire another important school was established during the period under consideration, a school which has also stood the test of time. An Episcopalian public school was established for the 'sons of Scottish gentry' who had only the option of 'Presbyterian education' heretofore. The school was further projected as a training college for Anglican theological students. Sited on the estate of the Rt. Hon George Patton (the Law Lord, Lord Glenalmond) of Cairnies, the school was to develop into Trinity College, Glenalmond. The chief founders of the school were Edward Bannerman Ramsay (1793-1872), Episcopalian Dean of Edinburgh, W.E. Gladstone, a Tractarian as well as a politician, and James R. Hope (later Hope-Scott) (1812-73), the parliamentary barrister, grandson of the second Earl of Hopetoun, and who married the grand-daughter of Sir Walter Scott. The foundation stone of Trinity College chapel was laid by Sir John Gladstone of Fasque (1764-1851), father of W.E. Gladstone, on 8 Sept 1846; the school was opened in May 1847.

On the death of Queen Victoria at Osborne House, Isle of Wight, in January 1901, Perth and Perthshire had gone a long way towards being 'Anglicised'. The upper strata of Perthshire society were increasingly being educated in English schools and universities and its commerce was steadily coming under the control of English-based capitalism. The new king, born Albert Edward, Prince of Wales, on 9 November 1841, was sixty years old when he succeeded his mother and because of her fear that he would turn out like her 'wicked uncles' (the sons of George III) she had kept him out of the administrative affairs of her realm. He was therefore not well-trained for his new job. In fact all that Edward really knew about his new kingdom was its contribution towards his vast appetite and sporting pleasures.

The age of Edward VII was a period of affluence and ostentation, of strict social discipline, of peace and plenty. It was also an age of unrest and poverty, of uncertainty about Britain's place in the world, as well as of growing concern that so very much was owned by so few. This short but intensely active period 1901-1910 was, in total, a time of transition between the leisurely self-confident Victorian Age, and the bursting revolutionary years which were to be heralded by the advent of World War I.

The industrial explosion of the Victorian era wrenched a large part of the rural society, that had predominated in Perthshire, away from the dominating traditions of the landed aristocracy. Politics too had been manipulated by men who, for the most part, derived their position from the fact that they owned property. Now a new social force was at work. Part of the nation's wealth was now earned in Perthshire, and the men who practiced it therein were beginning to exert their influence in government and other fields.

It was this economic necessity that forced the majority of Edward's subjects to move from rural areas to cities like Perth. The importation of cheap food from America and the Colonies made it impossible to grow food economically in Britain, with the result that the flow of agricultural workers into Perth, and the other larger towns in Perthshire, increased. So Edwardian Perth was bustling and bursting at the seams.

The street scenes depicted in this book show how the thoroughfares of the larger Perthshire towns of Victoria and Edward's days reflected the clutter of the average home. People went out from the early hours, the first afoot being the milk vendors and the bakers with their baskets of steaming baps, scones and pancakes. By 8 o'clock the itinerants were out: the knife-grinders, the pan menders and the home-produce sellers. It was a scene of noise with the wheels and horses of drays, carriages and carts being the noisiest. Busy, perhaps, but wages were low and distress was only too apparent; the extent was to be brought into focus by Conservative Prime Minister A.J. Balfour's Royal Commission on the Poor Law and the Relief of Distress.

Half of the houses in Edwardian Perth, and the towns and villages of the county, had still one or two rooms with shared extra-mural sanitation. Most were dark, draughty, cramped, malodorous and vermin infested. A two-roomed house could cost as much as 3/6 (17½p) per week, while a one-roomed cottage fetched 1/- (5p); a high sum for an 18/- (90p) a week unskilled worker. Wages were by no means equitable for physical work done; a full-time shop assistant might earn £30 per year, whereas a science master could command £140. But most people settled at the average 22/- (£1.10) a week pay of the farm worker.

The standard of living of Perthshire's well-to-do was dependant on a low rate of income tax (1/- in the £ above £160 per annum) and on the plentiful supply of domestic servants. 'Service' was an increasing field of employment for women in Edwardian Perthshire. A 'tweenie' in a 'big hoose' might earn £12 a year, with ambitions of the dizzy heights of housekeeper at £80 per year, while a boy, on £10 a year as a hallboy, might advance eventually to the £100 per year of a butler.

The Edwardian Age ended on 6 May 1910 when Edward VII died at a quarter to midnight at Buckingham Palace. By and large in that year the people of Perthshire were still earning less in real terms than they had in 1900. The ostentatious display of wealth and extravagance of Edward VII and his circle had left the lower classes resentful and dissatisfied, a feeling which was strong in the towns between worker and local gentry. The year of the king's death introduced three years of civil strife in the United Kingdom of an unprecedented scale, strife which was felt at grassroots level in Perthshire.

A Perthshire man or woman born in 1837 to die in 1910 would have seen many social changes. The spread of popular education, the enhanced mobility of new transport systems and the development of trade unionism, especially amongst the unskilled, made perhaps the most lasting effects. In Perthshire, too, were felt the movements which were gradually helping to forge Scotland into a single nation. The Liberal government's social and economic legislation gave Scotland a changing mood. Perth folk felt themselves more Scottish after generations of considering the modes and ideas of the Anglo-Saxon south. By 1910 there was a more clearly defined feeling that they were Celtic. In those days too the folk of Perthshire who were franchised believed that they could have an influence on national government. When in January 1910 the Liberal Alexander Frederick Whyte won the City of Perth he told his supporters in Perth Drill Hall: 'You have lighted a beacon which will shine brightly across broad Scotland, and no doubt some of those beams will find their way into the less enlightened corners of England.' Such optimism was to be dashed on the battlefields of Flanders only a few brief years later.

St Andrews, 1985   RAYMOND LAMONT-BROWN

CHAPTER ONE
A GALLERY OF CHARACTERS

4. George Dewar of West Park, a Perthshire keeper and his dogs. There was plenty of work for the Highland gamekeepers all the year round, especially during the official shooting season. During his first visit to Scotland with Queen Victoria, in 1842, Prince Albert went hunting with Lord Breadalbane and in one day shot nineteen roe deer, several hares and pheasants and three brace of grouse.

5. Charles McIntosh (1839-1922), sawmiller and postrunner,—the Inver naturalist—contemplates a winter scene in the company of his dog *Cailleach* (Gaelic for old wifie). During the winter of 1894-95 the lochs and streams were icebound for six weeks. In those days a whole ox was roasted on the ice to be washed down with whisky at 2/6d (12½p) a bottle.

6. Beatrix Potter with William Gaskill at Dalguise House, near Dunkeld, where Beatrix spent many happy summer holidays. It was from Dunkeld on 4 September 1894 that she wrote the famous letter about Peter Rabbit to Noel.

7. The bride goes to her wedding by bicycle? Not exactly, she was taking part in a Sports Day event at Laggan Park, Comrie, around 1910.

8.   Victorian studio portraiture has left us an important record of the civil servants of the day. Here Angus Crawford and Archibald Dougall, respectively Sheriff's Officer and Court Officer of Dunblane, pose in 1876 with the solemnity which they deemed befitting their station. The photograph was taken by one of the Stirlings of Kippendavie, a keen Victorian amateur photographer.

9. Every Perthshire town and village had its own characters and worthies. The Crieff eccentric, Sandy Merrie, who lived in Milnab Street, Crieff, sits for us here in this picture of around 1900.

Below left
10. In the days before the development of sophisticated media the local bellman was an important communicator. He gave public notice of all the new developments in an area. Our bellman cried the news in Blairgowrie.

Below right
11. The name of this Crieff worthy has not come down to us, but he is dressed for the sporting field of the 1860s and has a face that has seen many winters.

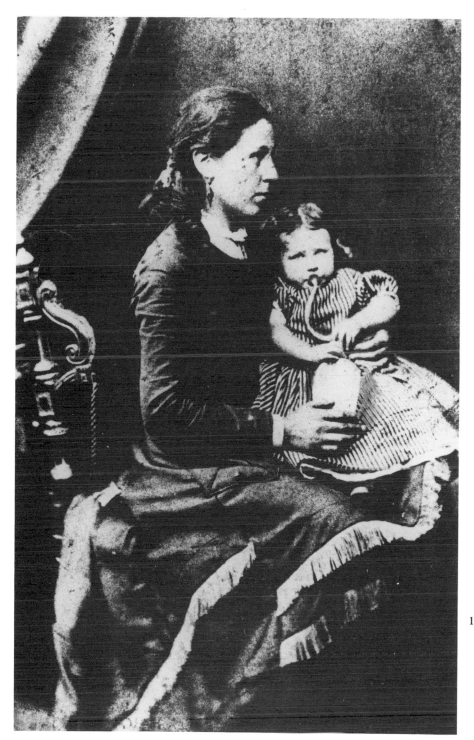

12. The earliest infant feeder dates back some two millennia BC. In the 19th century pottery gave place to glass. During 1867, one Captain Webber invented a feeding bottle which incorporated a thermometer to check the temperature of the contents. 'The Infant's Companion Feeder' with its long rubber tube and teat 'in best black India rubber' dates from 1900. Rubber teats did not come into use until the 1840s, and sucking tubes date from around 1864. In the better class homes some of the infant feeders were of cut glass, etched with sacred monograms. Our informant does not know the name of the sitters in this Victorian picture, but it is possible that they are of the Hally family of the Smiddie, Upper Allan St, Blairgowrie.

13. John Nish, tailor, of 36 Drummond St, Muthill. For such a workman hours were long, tasks were hard and the monetary rewards were few. A suit for 'Sunday best' cost £1.10s (£1.50) at the turn of the century and was made to last a lifetime. Circa 1910.

14. Kirsty Stewart gathers firewood with her young helper, Alistair Forbes, at Dunkeld. Around Dunkeld the afforestation stood as a tribute to the Dukes of Atholl. John, 4th Duke of Atholl (1755-1830) was the first to plant the larch (*Larix Europea*), introduced into Scotland in 1738.

CHAPTER TWO
DOWN HIGHWAYS AND BYEWAYS

15. The Mill on the Dochart, Killin, after a flood. The River Dochart flows from Loch Dochart, at the head of Glen Dochart, to Loch Tay, at Killin. At the foot of Stron-a-Chlachain, near the confluence of the 'roaring' Dochart and the 'gentle' Lochay, Killin is the oldest and the largest centre of population in the parish. On the small island of Inch Buie, on the River Dochart, was the burial place of the Clan MacNab, the most powerful family in the area until their emigration to Canada in the 19th century. The photograph is from the Valentine collection.

16. A tram passes the General Post Office, High St, Perth. The first site of the Post Office was at the head of George St and Charlotte St. Robert Anderson was appointed first postmaster of Perth in 1689, and the first stage-coach carrying the Royal Mail between Edinburgh and Perth began in 1799. The last tram ran in Perth on 19 January 1929.

17. Perth from Edinburgh Road. In the foreground is the line of the Edinburgh, Perth and Dundee railway. At the top left is H.M. Prison overlooking Merchant's Quay, Harbour Road and the tidal harbour. Barnhill and Kinnoull Hill lie to the right. In the middle distance is seen the spire of St John's Kirk. The city was extensively 'improved' in 1877 and 1893.

18. A corner of Dargie churchyard, Invergowrie, looking into Station Road. In this Wilson print of 4 May 1895 we see the cottage now greatly redeveloped; modern houses flank the trees to the right today, but the railings round the Cox memorial are still in position. Alexander Wilson was a calender (roller-machine for cloth) manufacturer who lived in Nethergate, Dundee. He was a semi-professional photographer who produced in excess of 5000 glass negatives. He died in 1923.

19. A Wilson Print of Kinfauns Ferry, 6 May 1896. Here the Carse of Gowrie begins and salmon fishing was once extensive hereabouts. In past times Kinfauns castle 'exercised a powerful jurisdiction' over the Tay.

20. Monorgan farm cottages, signal box and Longforgan station, circa 1895. This Wilson print is taken by the bridge over the Huntly Burn. The Dundee-Perth railway through Longforgan (the station was a mile away from the village) was opened 25 May 1847.

21. Victorians on an outing outside Longforgan Inn (now Longforgan Hotel) in this Wilson print of the mid-1890s. Next door to the inn was Moir's butchers where refreshments were served. The village's telegraph wires are clearly seen; payphones first appeared in shops in 1884 and the first payphone kiosks (of non-standard type) appeared in 1886. Perthshire's first standard kiosks did not appear until 1921.

22. James Square, Crieff, named after James, third Duke of Perth— or so Alexander Porteous avers in his *History of Crieff*. On the right stands the Murray Fountain of 1894, erected by the inhabitants of the burgh in recognition 'of many benefits received from the Murrays of Ochtertyre'. The gas lights are a prominent part of the street furniture; the Crieff Gas Company was formed in 1841. The *Temperance Hotel* is on the left, and the building with spire in the centre is the British Linen Bank (1880).

23. It is interesting to compare this picture of James Square, Crieff, in 1857, with the one above, The burgh boundaries of Crieff were fixed in 1863 and the Commissioners for the Burgh of Crieff first met in 1864. A town hall was erected here in 1850 and a post office in 1906.

24. Crieff *en fête* to celebrate the 21st birthday of William Keith Murray of Ochtertyre, 8 April 1893, the son of Sir Patrick Keith Murray Bt. Sir Patrick had assured a water supply for Crieff from his estates (the Loch Turret scheme, 1873) and to mark this and the coming of age mentioned, the Murray Fountain was erected in 1894.

25. Victorian Scone. Until 1805 the village of Scone stood close to the Palace. Then the second Earl of Mansfield decided to have the village moved some mile and a half away to benefit expansion, thus Old Scone and New Scone came about. The electric tramway between Perth and Scone was opened in 1905, but there had been a horse-drawn tram from 1895. The fare was 1d.

26. A glimpse down the Main Street, Comrie, around 1860. The seismic observatory on top of Brough and Macpherson's building is a prominent feature. Comrie has always been famous for its earthquakes, as the highland boundary fault lies to the south of the village. The first recorded earthquake centred on Comrie took place 5 November 1789 and further smaller tremors were felt up to the 'great earthquake' of 23 October 1839. This phenomena aroused the interest of local inhabitants, and in the early 1800s a small group formed themselves into the Comrie Pioneers to study local earthquakes. In the 1830s they averred to have studied some 7300 tremors from the observatory. The group pioneered instruments for recording and measuring the tremors and the first seismometer was designed and made for them in 1841 by Professor J.D. Forbes of Edinburgh. The owner of the shop in Comrie's Main Street, above which the observatory was placed, was one Peter MacFarlane, postmaster, who was responsible for the building. He stands in the foreground wearing striped trousers. The observatory was removed later in the century. After a fire in 1903 the then owner of the site Mr P. Mackintosh engaged Charles Rennie Mackintosh to draw up plans for the present building.

27. J. Stewart's Commercial Hotel, Comrie; the building dates from 1862. Note the 'mashers' (a late-Victorian word to describe flirtatious dandies) with their bowlers and walking-canes. The hotel sign declares the sale of porter, a popular Victorian dark brown malt liquor.

28. The Doghead Well, Willoughby St., Muthill. The village was once a favourite haunt of tinkers who set up their winter camps at Findale and Balloch. The distinctive oil lamps for street lighting are worthy of mention. Note too, the cast iron pump once a very common sight in Scottish villages. Tom McCromie is seen here with the mail coach en route to Greenloaning station, circa 1905.

29. St Fillans, Parish of Comrie, circa 1844; note the thatched roofs of the cottages. A quiet scene before the development of tourism following Queen Victoria's visit of 1842.

30. Alyth, circa 1910. The Alyth Burn flows through the town and is spanned by 10 bridges within the burgh boundaries. Spinning was the major industry up to the late 1890s, and then raspberry and potato growing with some weaving.

31. The Round Tower, Abernethy. The mists of antiquity obscure the origins of the tower. Some authorities attribute it to around the end of the eleventh century; others believe that it belongs to an earlier period and that it was a lookout tower during the Danish invasions. Whatever its origins, it was a popular subject for Victorian photographers.

32. Private hire carriages assembled in Kenmore Square outside the west entrance to Taymouth Castle, 1896, home of the Earls of Breadalbane and Holland. In 1837, the earl introduced from Sweden the capercailzie, which had become extinct in Scotland. The building on the left is known as the Library. In 1842 Queen Victoria visited the castle as a guest of the second Marquess and fifth Earl of Breadalbane who died in 1862.

33. Coupar Angus, on the eastern fringe of Perthshire, is in the heart of Strathmore. Until 1891 part of Coupar Angus parish was in the old County of Forfar. The town hall was built to commemorate Queen Victoria's Jubilee and cost around £4000; the Queen visited the town in 1844.

34. Blairgowrie Station at the turn of the century. The opening of the branch line of the Scottish Midland Junction Railway on 28 July 1855 was received with some apathy in the town. As the *Statistical Account of Scotland* tells us: 'There was no demonstration, no flag waving, no shouts and no wish expressed that the Blairgowrie Branch Railway would flourish'. The local train was called the 'Blairie' and ran to Dundee.

35. Situated at the foothills of the Grampians, Blairgowrie was once known for its spinning industry, but most of the men seen in this picture taken near the fountain (1893) at Wellmeadow would be employed by Greenbank Engineering Works (1876). As seen in this photograph, street lighting was sparse; a Gas Works had been set up in 1834 and gas lighting in the streets continued until 1930.

36. A roof-mender with tiles balanced precariously on his head is the real focal point of this picture taken in Commercial Street, Blairgowrie in the reign of Edward VII. Up to 1901 Blairgowrie had two town councils; one under the influence of the 'superior' of the town and the other under the General Police & Improvements (Scotland) Act, 1862, adopted in 1876.

37. Local children play at The Cross, Dunkeld. The Dairy on the right was owned by Mrs Irvine who was famed for her girdle scones. In 1853, Anne, Duchess of Atholl (d.1897) established an industrial school for girls at The Cross.

38. Birnham Hotel, circa 1900, from a Wilson print. In the parish of Little Dunkeld, Birnham was long known for its forests and developed as a tourist area with the coming of the railway in 1856. The Birnham Hotel was built by Sir William Stewart of Murthly, but was completely destroyed by fire in 1912; it was rebuilt in 1913.

39. Farmer's boy with spring cart at the Loch of the Lowes, Dunkeld. Good trout fishing abounded in this area as well as catches of pike. Many a fisherman lingered here in the hope of landing a Tay salmon.

40. Schoolchildren pose for the camera in Duchess Street, Stanley, outside Mrs McFarlane's wine and spirit house (1800) at the turn of the century. The village owed its origins to the building of a cotton spinning mill in the 1780s by Richard Arkwright and his partners.

41. Thatched dry-stone cottage at Tigh-na-leacain ('the house of the cheek of the burn'), Aberfeldy, adjacent to the military road established by General Wade. The barrow is of the type used for wheeling in the peats. Many people lived in such dark, smoky, insanitary biggins during 1837-1910. The means of lighting within was first the traditional crusie and thereafter the paraffin lamp.

42. Children loll and adults stroll in the sunshine in this late-Victorian print by Wilson of Bankfoot, in the parish of Auchtergaven. Bankfoot is a long village on the edge of the level Cairnleith Moss. People would come from the outlying farms to spend a day in the village and many shopkeepers offered 'Teas and Light Refreshments' all the year round.

43. Ballinluig Post Office on the Great North Road in the 1890s. The old 'Boat Road' to the one time Tummel Ferry leads off to the left. Some five or six postmen, a post girl and telegram messengers served the district from this post office. The inn at the centre back was where staging horses were changed; up to 1879 toll-gates barred the road. It is said that John Brown had an altercation with a villager who shone his lamp on Queen Victoria's face, in the 1860s, while her horses were being changed here.

44. Taken around 1900, this photograph looks towards Ben-y-Vrackie from a point on the road opposite the present Pitlochry High School. The man at the corner of the road is William Robertson of the Pitlochry Drapery Co; he later emigrated to South Africa.

45. Craigower Hotel, Pitlochry, 22 August 1903. The hotel sign offers a welcome to cyclists. The bicycle had been introduced to Scotland in the 1860s, and became a craze in the 1890s. Cycle touring clubs visited such hotels as this.

46. The High Street, Dunblane, 1904. the mud had regularly to be scraped to the side of the unsurfaced roadway. To the left of the street musician with his tin whistle are two boys . . . one is the late Johnny Maillie, while on his right, wearing a white collar, is the late Robert MacAlpine (d. 1984) then about twelve years of age. Mr MacAlpine . . . the renowned 'Ting a' Leerie' . . . was the former proprietor of MacAlpine's Stores which his mother started around 1901. At the top of the High Street lies the town jail and the police station, erected in 1842 on the site of the old town house of Viscount Strathallan. The old jail was demolished in 1963.

47. The Stirling Arms, once a noted coaching station after its extension in 1900. The gateway to the left and its accompanying lodge and drive were erected in 1854 and led to Kippenross House the home of the Stirlings of Kippendavie. Robert Burns visited the inn in 1787.

48. A popular scenic spot on the River Dochart at Killin. From around the 1880s a number of larger houses were built with a small cottage at the rear. The idea was to let the big house for the summer months while the family lived in the cottage. Killin was a holiday resort then for wealthy families from the cities who might take such a house for three months. The view here, caught by a Victorian photographer, has possibly been painted by artists more often than any other scene in Scotland. For the foaming Dochart, gurgling and splashing over its rocky bed, gives a touch of life to the landscape bounded by the highland hills. This section is started and finished with views from the collection of Messrs Valentine & Sons of Dundee. The firm was originated in 1826 by James Valentine, a lithographer, who added photography to his business in 1850; Valentine became a photographic publisher about 1860. In later years Valentines promoted their postcard publishing enterprise and were well represented when the postcard had its 'golden age' between 1870 and 1930.

CHAPTER THREE

WORKING THE LAND

DURING THE whole of the period covered by this book, Perthshire depended predominantly on its agriculture and land utilisation. The county, the fourth largest in Scotland, presented the Victorian and Edwardian tourist with clear contrasts: the arable land, permanent grass land and the woodland of the lowlands of Strathmore, Strathearn and the Carse of Gowrie, and some of the valley bottoms on the one hand, and the heathland, moorland and rough pasture of the Highlands on the other.

The problems of making a livelihood from agriculture in Perthshire varied from parish to parish and with the topographical features of the area. From the deep loam soils of the Tay to the less fertile Grampians, the farms were representative of all forms of crops and stock production. By the time Victoria came to the throne the agricultural revolution was well under way in Perthshire and the years 1840-70 saw a 'golden age' of agriculture with innovative practices changing the feudal system of husbandry which had prevailed for centuries. During these days too, many fine farmhouses and steadings were built in Perthshire.

In 1838 Hugh Watson Keiller of Coupar Angus purchased ten heifers and a bull at Trinity Fair, Brechin, thus making the foundation of a fine Aberdeen-Angus herd. Today Perthshire is the homeland of Aberdeen-Angus and Beef Shorthorn cattle. In 1827 Patrick Bell, a divinity student from Auchterhouse, Angus, invented a reaper which was later recognised for its worth. What happened in agriculture in Perthshire had far reaching results nationally.

£100 REWARD.

STOLEN, between 12th August and 1st November, 1895, from the forest of Clunie (Laighwood Grazings), Perthshire :—

60 BLACKFACED EWES of different Ages, marked as follows–
LUG MARKS—Top off right Lug ; two Nips on left Lug.
HORNBURN—"R" on right Horn, with age figure 1 to 5 ; also, Saw marks on Horns.
BUIST—"C" on left side with tar.

Also, between the end of July and 17th October, 1895, — probably about beginning of October, — from the Hill Pastures of Auchlyne and Croftchose, Killin :—

206 BLACKFACED EWES, marked as follows,--
LUG MARKS—Back half both Lugs, or back half right Lug and Nip above left Lug.
HORNBURN—"G.C." or "J.C."
BUIST—"A." on near side with tar.

The Perthshire Association for the Prevention of Sheep Stealing offer the above Reward to any person giving such information to either of the undersigned as will lead to the recovery of the Stolen Sheep, and conviction of the thief, or in proportion to the number recovered.

JOHN CAMPBELL, Woodlands, Crieff.
R. A. ROBERTSON, Banker, Killin.
ALEX. MACBETH, Writer, Pitlochry.

A. M'DONALD & Son, Printers, Crieff.

50. Mrs McGregor milking at Acharn cow park, in the parish of Kenmore, 1896. By this time dairy farming was well-developed in Perthshire and the regular supply of 'pure rich milk' was a desirable service in pre-refrigeration days.

51. Muck-spreading at Lochearnhead, 1888. The cycle of farming was very effective: the better the muck, the better the crops; the better the quality of the crops, the more cattle could feed; the better the cattle, the better the muck.

52. Haymaking on the manse glebe, Kenmore. Loch Tay is in the background. In past days each kirk manse had a glebe (a field) which was set aside for the clergyman's benefice. As time went by, these glebes were 'let out' to local farmers.

53. A ploughing match at Weem, north of the Tay, near Aberfeldy, in 1901. The ploughing and horsemanship skills of these farm workers always drew crowds at these annual matches among the folk of Weem who were described as 'healthy, honest, hard-working and thrifty'.

54. The traction engine *Big Mill* hauls a threshing machine from Dunkeld to Birnham. Threshing time was a great social occasion for a system of 'loan days' was in operation when one farmer helped another.

55. A haymaking scene at Strathallan Castle, circa 1860. On the right of the picture stand three of the daughters of the laird, the Hon. William Henry Drummond, namely, Fanny, Hersey and Minnie. Haymaking tools were still primitive and the work labour-intensive.

56. Reaping near Lawers, in the parish of Kenmore, Sept 1902. Horses were the great motive power on the Victorian and Edwardian Perthshire farm. In 1894 there were 221 horses kept in the parish for work purposes; seventy years later there were less than forty which were mostly kept for pleasure.

57. Tar-branding to establish ownership. The scene is thought to be Remony estate, Acharn, parish of Kenmore, circa 1898. At that time the land belonged to the Earl of Breadalbane of Taymouth Castle.

CHAPTER FOUR
ON THE ROAD

THE ORIGINS OF the Scottish tinker are lost in unrecorded time and can hardly be reconstructed today. The attitudes of the Perthshire tinkers were coloured to a considerable degree by the opinions of outsiders towards them. In spite of the draconian measures to get rid of them, from the time of James VI, the tinkers survived. Perthshire was one place where tinkers were harshly treated; in Auchterarder, for instance, they were whipped, branded, expelled and executed at regular intervals throughout the Middle Ages.

By the coming of Victoria's reign the tinkers were a wandering group which travelled the roads, usually with a covered cart drawn by a lean horse. On a rainy night their curious tents would be huddled by a loch or burnside, with a hissing fire at the door. Usually the tinkers went around in family groups. Tinkers were not circumscribed by wedding ceremonial. If a young man and a girl wished to marry they simply moved into a tent together. Marriage only became useful with the coming of Social Welfare payments. The tinkers spoke their own language referred to as 'the cant'.

Obsequiousness and wheedling were the major traits of the tinkers and they won a living collecting rags, begging, doing farm work, peddling, telling fortunes and horse-dealing. At Blairgowrie they were involved in raspberry picking. Often the tinkers met with physical aggression if they tried to involve themselves with church, or school, and invariably they were moved on by the authorities and were accused of local thefts. By and large the populace treated them with fear and there was nothing too bad to accuse them of . . . from body-snatching to child-stealing.

58. Overcome by John Barleycorn, this tinker sleeps it off at the roadside, Loch Tay, 1907. Drunkenness was categorised by the Church of Scotland as the main moral cause of poverty in the report presented in 1910 to the Royal Commission on the Poor Law and the Relief of Distress. In 1907 beer cost 1½d (½p) per pint, and whisky 3s (15p) per bottle.

59. A tinker encampment along Loch Tayside, 1907. Some tinkers camped in groups, others in family units. Usually tinkers were considered to be totally independent of marriage. They did not believe even in temporary hospitalisation should sickness occur.

60. A tinker family group photographed by the salmon-rich waters of Loch Tay, 1907. Children were generally well-treated by their tinker parents; even so, schooling was considered valueless apart from its provision of the rudimentary writing skills.

CHAPTER FIVE

VEHICLES GREAT AND SMALL

THE PICTURES in this section show the wide variety of vehicles still in use in Perthshire up to 1910. The rapid growth in the number of cars, and the improved performance of the vehicles had a disastrous effect on Perthshire's untarred roads, and in spite of increased public demand it was many years before the main roads were macadamised. The first motor car, a Benz was introduced to Britain in 1894 and with it came the motor car hobby. By 1896 the Locomotives on Highways Act removed many of the restrictions on road transport imposed by the notorious 'Red Flag Act' of 1878 and now the speed limit was raised to 14mph. By the turn of the century the horse bus gave way to the motor bus. The greatest change of all however came with the 1914–18 war. The railways entered a long decline hit by the loss of middle-class passengers to the motor car; again freight went to goods lorries and working class passengers to the charabanc. The tram was hit too and soon totally disappeared from the streets.

61. Lochearnhead coach at St Fillans with coachman, Cameron, August 1889. Railway companies and hotels had their own carriages to ferry passengers to and from rail links. Privately owned horses and carriages required stabling, coachmen and grooms and the need for a large labour force throughout Victorian and Edwardian times.

62. Boat of Caputh. Because of its position this parish was somewhat isolated, but the ferry across to the mainline of traffic to the south ensured its importance. A parish church was built here in 1500 and a steeple was added in 1865. The ferry was replaced by a bridge constructed from undamaged spans from the ill-fated Tay rail bridge at Dundee.

63. Burnmouth Ferry, Stanley, on the River Tay 1899. Stretches of the river hereabouts, below Campsie Linn, provided some of the best salmon fishing in Scotland.

64. Taking up a position at the end of Scott Street, Mr Stewart shows off his expanding family and his cart. Possession of one's own horse-drawn transport was a mark of social status. It is interesting to note that a horse ate 6 tons of food a year and by 1902 there were 3.5 million horses in Britain.

65. The first motor bus service began in Edinburgh in 1898 and the idea rapidly caught on. Here a local motor bus waits for passengers at Pitlochry.

66. Baird, the barber, Jack Scotland (of Scotland's Hotel), MacAra, who worked at Russell's Garage, Pitlochry, and McRae, the driver, pose in this pre-1914 Argyll saloon.

67. A display of Ford motor cars, circa 1905, Aberfeldy. The firm of Nicol & Wood became that of McKerracher which ran buses in the area as far as Perth. The showroom is now the lounge of the Crown Hotel. Driving tests were not introduced until 1935.

68. The Victorians always equated the railways with progress and civilization. The railways brought to Perthshire a whole new range of buildings and engineering works became a part of the Perthshire landscape from tunnels to viaducts, but the most memorable has been the railway station. The foundation stone of the General Railway Station was laid at Perth in 1847 only a short time after the Dundee to Perth railway had opened. Here a very early locomotive of the Caledonian Railway sets off from Perth.

69. Horse trams pass each other in the High Street, Perth. In the background is the old Post Office. To the left is Stead & Simpson's boot store and the National Restaurant at the junction with Kinnoull Street. The horse trams gave way to electric cars on Tuesday, 31 October 1905.

70. The Aberfeldy-Kenmore charabanc stands outside Aberfeldy Station. This was a vital link in the Loch Tay Steamers service. The vehicle's registration is a Lanarkshire one.

71. The wreck of the steamer, *Alma,* at Aberfeldy, 1873. The lade that ran under the road at Aberfeldy gave way under the weight of the steamer and the vessel was shipwrecked in Bank St. The yacht had been ordered by the Earl of Breadalbane but it is said that it was never used as the earl and his family were afraid of water. Eventually the ship was moored in Loch Tay, west of the bridge at Kenmore, and so deteriorated that in time it sank. There are those who still remember the rigging sticking out of the water.

72. The traction engine which pulled the steamer, *Alma,* from Glasgow to Aberfeldy (the yacht had been brought from the Isle of Wight). Aberfeldy 1873.

CHAPTER SIX

SHIPS AND SAILING

The Loch Tay Steamers sailed between Killin (Loch Tay Pier), where connections were made with the Killin Railway (a branch of the Caledonian, later LMS) and Kenmore. Near Kenmore there was a small shipyard where the steamers were based and overhauled. The Earl, later the Marquess, of Breadalbane, a director of the Caledonian Railway Co., played a large part in the establishment of regular services on both Loch Awe and Loch Tay. The intention was that the steamers would make connections with the Caledonian trains as required and expand tourism.

In 1882 the Earl (as he was at that date) created the Loch Tay Steamboat Co., which in 1922 was taken over by the Caledonian Steam Packet Co., the marine subsidiary of the Caledonian Railway Co., and in 1923 came under the control of the newly-formed London, Midland and Scottish Railway Co., and a total of six steamers plied on the loch. Two of these were large passenger vessels, employed in the summer tourist trade: one was a small passenger vessel, suitable for use in the winter, one was used mainly for cargo, but could also carry passengers, and one was purely a cargo vessel. The sixth was Lord Breadalbane's private yacht, which also might be pressed into passenger service if necessary.

The following five vessels formed the Loch Tay Steamboat Company fleet. The two large passenger steamers were constructed partly or wholly in the builders' yard on the Clyde, taken to Loch Tay in sections, and then re-assembled there. At least two of the remainder, and probably all three were built of local timber on the shores of the loch at Acharn.

Five steamers are particularly remembered on this route:

LADY OF THE LAKE:1882-1927. 68GT. Built by Anderson & Lyall, Govan, with engines by D. Rowan & Co, Glasgow. She was an Iron Screw steamer.

SYBILLA:1882-1927. 37GT. D. Fenton of Perth built this Wood Screw steamer with Rowan engines.

QUEEN OF THE LAKE: 1907-50. 152GT. Ailsa Shipbuilding Co. Ltd, Ayr built this Steel Screw steamer.

CARLOTTA: 1883-1923. 22GT. A. Gifford of Leith built her with engines by Ross & Duncan. Used sometimes by Lord Breadalbane as his yacht.

MAGPIE: 1882-1907. Wood Single Screw.

73.   The *Lady of the Lake* makes her way to Kenmore pier. Summer sailings were maintained until 1939. The route from Killin to Kenmore took in Ardeonaig, Lawers, Ardtalnaig and Fearnan.

74. A North Sea trader, *The Bravo,* probably one of the Baltic ships, lies at anchor at Perth, circa 1873. These ships were so large that they had to be pulled to a berth by tug. During the early years of Victoria's reign several plans were put forward for the construction of a better harbour at Perth and the deepening of the river channel. Little or nothing was done except, when the railway bridge was built in 1863, it was devised that the bridge would swing open to allow tall ships like *The Bravo* to pass. By 1848 some 486 ships were visiting Perth harbour; the harbour had shrunk in importance since the Middle Ages. Undoubtedly the sea trade suffered from the advent of the railway.

75. The paddle-steamer, *Lass O'Gowrie,* lies alongside the quay at Perth. The ship was used both for towage and
summer traffic and plied the Tay from Perth to Dundee, and sometimes to the Bridge of Earn. She belonged to
David Edwards and was sold to Cosens of Weymouth. She plied 1883-89 on the Tay and changed her name to
Albert Victor on being sold. She remained in existence until 1928.

CHAPTER SEVEN
SPORT AND LEISURE

76. A sporting party at Inchbrakie, 1863, the home of Patrick Graeme, whose father married the daughter of James, Viscount Strathallan. In the picture are: The Hon. Elizabeth Edwardes, Capt. Davidson, Capt. The Hon. W. and Louisa Edwardes, Mr Derby, Capt. the Hon. Arthur and Mrs Hay Drummond. Playing games in crinolines must have been very difficult.

77. Perth Bridge during a hard Victorian winter. The houses of Rosemount and Tayhill rise to the left. People skate, walk and stroll while others are confident enough to take chairs onto the ice.

78. Scone Curling Club. Note the equipment, the stones, the brushes and the footmats. Curling evolved in the Lowlands of Scotland from a rough trial of strength with misshapen boulders. The Royal Caledonian Curling Club was formed in 1838.

79. Humphrey Christie of the Dunkeld Cycle Club, circa 1890. Christie was a grocer by trade and was a very keen amateur rider who had great success and won many trophies and medals, a few of which are displayed here.

80. Victorian photographs tend to be formal, but there are some telling studies of character seen in such groups as this. Perth Band, Fechney Industrial School. The Industrial School was situated in Glasgow Rd and in 1889 the bandmaster was G.W. Large. By 1872 music featured in the curriculum of most schools. Private music making was one of the major leisure activities of the period.

81. The brass band was one of the most distinctive products of Victorian music culture. The smartly uniformed bandsmen playing martial music were a familiar part of everyday life. They provided entertainment in the public parks and headed most parades. Here a band at Coupar Angus shows off a range of instruments.

82. A visit of the Edinburgh Cycle Club to Clathie House, Comrie, 1875. By the 1890s cycling was a craze and Cycling Touring Clubs mushroomed. Until the 'safety bicycle' was introduced in the 1880s, cycling was a male activity as the high bicycles, or 'ordinaries' were dangerous and totally unsuitable for long skirts.

83. A middle-class family on a day's outing to Strathyre, August 1889. The photograph was taken by J.E.A. Steggall, Professor of Mathematics in the University of St Andrews. Most well-to-do families had their own equipage of carriage and groom.

84. The Children's Holiday Home, Pitlochry. The home was founded by Mrs St. John Mildmay when she was Miss Gwyer of Croftinloan. Here relays of poor children from the city could be accommodated in healthy surroundings.

85. The MacDuff Institute was established under the Trusts of the Will of Archibald Campbell MacDuff as a Home for Boys. A squad of these boys is being taken for a highland dancing lesson by their Instructor, Pipe-Major A. Gordon. The buildings of the institute are in the background.

86. Children from the Royal School of Dunkeld, then sited at Culloden House (1891), paddle in the Tay. The seven-arch bridge built by Thomas Telford in 1809 is in the background. The bridge tollgates were removed in 1879.

87. Mrs J.B. McKenzie entertaining school pupils in the manse grounds. Mrs McKenzie, the wife of the minister, was a keen photographer. Loch Tay and Kenmore Church lie in the background.

88. Maggie Glencross and other children sledge on Brae St, Dunkeld. The stepped houses have long been demolished. The visible thackstones on the chimneyheads of the houses would suggest that these buildings were once thatched.

89. The Dunblane Ladies Golf Team outside the old club house at the foot of Laighill Loan in 1906. A nine-hole course was laid out on the Laighills in 1892 by Mr Philp of the Hydropathic (1878). The opening match took place between old Tom Morris of St Andrews and Bernard Sayers of North Berwick, in which they were beaten by two local players Leslie Balfour and Alexander Stuart. The course continued in use until 1923 when the present course was opened.

90. Andrew Murray curls with Lord Strathallan, 1864. Members of the Drummond family and others look on. The game is taking place somewhere near Strathallan Castle, Machany Water, some three miles southwest of Auchterarder. At Strathallan there were artificial curling ponds.

91. The mile handicap at Morrison's Academy grounds, Crieff. Modern British athletics began at Oxford in the 1850s. In 1880 there was the foundation of the Amateur Athletics Association which allowed the participation of working-class athletes. Like other sports running was thought to be good not only for the health but for character. The Academy was opened in 1860.

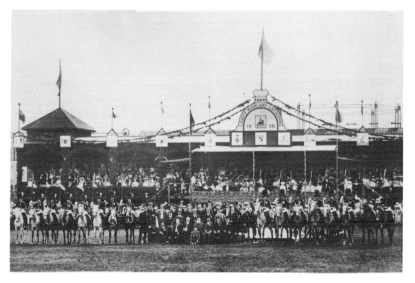

92. Crieff Highland Gathering, 1906. In time of war each of the Scottish clans had a gathering ground for rendezvous; eventually these gatherings led to the peaceful pursuit of games. The first Crieff Highland Games was held in the grounds of Morrison's Academy, 1870-78, and thence in the Market Park.

93. The Dancing Bear outside Stewart's Dental Surgery, Brown Street, Blairgowrie. Street entertainment had been popular from medieval times; exotic animals always drew the crowds in the largely unsophisticated society of rural Perthshire. Another favourite crowd-puller in Victorian times were the 'blackamoors', coloured musicians and tumblers from circuses.

CHAPTER EIGHT
MEN AT ARMS

94. H.M. King Edward VII arrives at Blairgowrie station on his way to lay the foundation stone of the Queen Victoria
School, Dunblane, 1908. Officers and men of the 5th Perthshire Highland Volunteers Battalion of the Black
Watch form the ceremonial welcoming party. Behind the king, his brother, HRH Prince Arthur, Duke of
Connaught, leads the military aides.

95. A soldier of the 5th Perthshire Highland Volunteers of the Black Watch lays out his kit for the daily inspection. The picture was taken sometime before 1908 and on top of the kit is seen a distinctive hat, a relic of the Boer War.

96. Almost bursting out of his uniform, General MacDuff of Bonhard, with his negro valet. Negro servants were long known in Scotland and were particularly employed in the 18th century. The Bonhard estates were sold in 1936.

97. This group, outside the front entrance to Blair Castle, is composed of Atholl Highlanders. The second from the left is John, the 7th Duke of Atholl.

98. Sergeants of the Atholl Highlanders at Blair Castle, 1884.
The regiment was raised as part of the British Army to fight
in the American War of Independence in 1777, but was
disbanded three years later. It was re-formed in 1839 by
Lord Glenlyon and acted as bodyguard to Queen Victoria
during her stay at Blair Castle in 1844. In 1845 colours were
presented on behalf of Queen Victoria by Lady Glenlyon.
The guard still exists and is the sole survivor of the ancient
custom whereby the King of Scotland had no army but
relied on local chiefs to bring their clan forces to support
them in time of war. Today it remains the last private army
in Europe.

99. Dan McGregor, cabinetmaker, wistfully poses in a photographic studio in his 'uniform'. His kit and percussion rifle
are thought to have been assembled from the photographer's
'stock'—such symbolic representations were not unusual
from the time of the Boer War, 1899-1902.

100. An officer of the local regiment, the Scottish Horse Regiment, in Bridge St, Dunkeld. The regiment was gazetted 15 Dec 1900, and the command was given to Capt. the Marquess of Tullibardine by Lord Kitchener; the corps was recruited from Scots in S. Africa. The guidons (pennants) of the regiment are laid up in Dunkeld cathedral.

CHAPTER NINE
PERTHSHIRE GENTRY

DURING THE one hundred and seventy years covered by this book, the lifestyle of the Perthshire gentry was a phenomenon without parallel anywhere in the world. The average Perthshire country house was the home of two societies, the servants and the served, who co-existed for each others welfare, one being dependent on the other. The 'big hoose' brought employment to the scattered villages and 'open house' was kept for hosts of relatives and friends who constantly came and went. In this selection of pictures we see the house parties and the men and women who made up polite society.

101. The Drummond family at Strathallan Castle. From left to right are: Miss Elliot, Hon. Mrs J.R. Drummond, Fanny Drummond, Admiral Drummond who fought in the Crimea, Miss Lee Mainwaring, Alice Drummond, Alpin MacGregor, Hersey Drummond, Miss Graeme of Inchbrakie and Lord Strathallan.

102.

THE HALDANES OF GLENEAGLES

Gleneagles House, the ancient family home and private estate of the Haldane family. The oldest part of the house is Jacobean having a detached pavilion and linking passageway. It was probably built by Sir John Haldane of that Ilk. The name Gleneagles, used in isolation, belongs solely to the Haldane family lands and is thought to be derived from the Gaelic *Eigeis,* meaning church. The name was misappropriated by the Caledonian Railway Company some sixty years ago and misused to add status to their new Hotel and Golf Courses in spite of strong protests by the Haldane family and the fact that the Gleneagles Hotel and Golf Courses are actually situated in Strathearn.

In the lower photograph can be seen the chapel of Gleneagles House from the North. There was an ecclesiastical building on this site from time immemorial. The chapel was restored in the 1930s by General Sir Aylmer Haldane and stands on the probable site of St Mungo's Cell. On the left is the lime avenue planted to commemorate the victorious Battle of Camperdown, 1797.

103.

104. Blair Castle, 1899. Thought to be a gathering to celebrate the return of the Marquess of Tullibardine and his wife from their honeymoon in Belgium. The Marquess was John George Stewart-Murray, who became 8th Duke of Atholl; he married Katherine Marjorie Ramsay, daughter of Sir James Ramsay of Bamff. Her Grace subsequently became MP for West Perthshire. Blair Castle remains the ancient home and fortress of the Dukes of Atholl. In the centre of the doorway stands the 7th Duke, who engaged John Bryce to recastellate his family home.

105. Louisa Moncrieffe, wife of the 7th Duke of Atholl in 1885. She was the daughter of Sir Thomas Moncrieffe. During her husband's time, the duke reverted to the original form of spelling of the title (Atholl instead of Athole).

106. Duchess Anne, wife of the 6th Duke of Athole, with basket carriage. She was Anne Home-Drummond, only daughter of Henry Home-Drummond of Blair Drummond. She was Lady-in-Waiting to Queen Victoria.

107. The Drummond family at Strathallan Castle. Mrs G. Home-Drummond stands on the left with Hon. Hersey Drummond, the Hon. Alice Drummond, the Hon. R. Melville, Emily Melville, Mr & Mrs Williamson of Lawers and a groom.

108.

THE MURRAYS OF SCONE

The Murrays have been living at Scone for nearly four centuries since the estates were granted to Sir David Murray of Gospetrie, Master of the King's Stable. The title of Mansfield was achieved by William Murray (d.1793), a lawyer who rose to be Chancellor of the Exchequer and Lord Chief Justice in 1757. He was created 1st Earl of Mansfield in Nottingham in 1776 and 1st Earl of Mansfield in Middlesex in 1792. David William Murray (1777-1840), 3rd Earl of Mansfield, gave the palace its present form, employing from 1802-12 the architect, William Atkinson. Herein Atkinson created a new 'Gothick palace' in which many of the rooms revealed a strong monastic influence of the former Abbey of Scone. Victoria stayed at Scone Palace in September 1842 as a guest of the 4th Earl; the Dowager Lady Mansfield (Frederica, widow of the 3rd Earl) acted as hostess. The Queen made a tour of the grounds of the palace and noted: 'Before our windows stands a sycamore tree planted by James VI'. The rooms used by the Queen are now on display to the public. She was given a curling lesson on the 168ft long polished wood floor of the Long Gallery as it was not the time of year for ice. The picture of the palace dates from the 1880s and is by James Valentine of Dundee.

'The royal city of Scone' was once the centre and capital of an area whose former importance is only marked today by the castellated palace, home of the Earls of Mansfield. At Scone, kings of Scotland were at first inaugurated and later crowned, and the earliest national councils were held here from the time of the Pictish High Kings of Scotland. The Abbey of Scone was burned down by a hysterical mob at the Reformation. The last coronation to take place at Scone was that of King Charles II in 1651. The youthful monarch stayed at 'the House of Scone', which forms the main structure of the palace today.

109. The bridal party assembled at the marriage of the Hon. Alan David Murray (1864-1935), and later 6th Earl of Mansfield, to Miss Margaret Helen MacGregor, daughter of Rear-Admiral Sir Malcolm MacGregor of MacGregor, Chief of the Clan Gregor. The wedding took place on 20 April 1899, at the then seat of the MacGregors, Edinchip, Lochearnhead.

110. The 4th Earl of Mansfield surrounded by family and friends at Scone Palace. They include Lord Stormont, his sons, The Hon. William Murray, The Hon. Angus Murray, The Hon. Andrew Murray, his daughter, Lady Mabel Murray. Herein too are Miss Margaret Helen MacGregor (later wife of the 6th Earl), her mother Lady MacGregor of MacGregor, The Duke and Duchess of Atholl and several members of the Steuart-Fotheringham family.

111. Kinpurnie Castle, Newtyle, Angus, in its first form, 1909. The building was altered in 1910. It was built for the 1st Sir Charles Cayzer on Keillor Hill by architect, Patrick Thoms. Sir Charles Cayzer (1843-1916), the 1st baronet was head of the firm of Cayzer, Irvine & Co. Ltd, the steamship owners. He sat as Conservative M.P. for Barrow-in-Furness, 1892-1906.

112. Family group outside Gartmore House, parish of Port of Monteith; the house was bought by Sir Charles Cayzer around 1900. Left to right the figures are: Sir Charles William Cayzer, 3rd baronet, Conservative M.P. for the City of Chester, 1922-40. Next, Sir Charles's fiancée, Eileen Meakin (d. 1981), the family nurse, the Dowager Lady Cayzer (formerly Agnes Elizabeth Trickey, widow of the 1st Sir Charles Cayzer, d.1919) and her companion/secretary. Then comes Lt.Com. Sir August Cayzer (1876-1943), 3rd son of the 1st baronet and second chairman of the Clan Line, holding his nephew, George Patrick John Rushmore (the present Earl Jellicoe). Seated are: Lady Lucy Jellicoe (b.1903, later Lady Lucy Latham), Lady Norah Jellicoe (b. 1910, later Lady Norah Wingfield), Bernard Cayzer (1914-81), and William Nicholas Cayzer (b.1910), the present Lord Cayzer of St Mary Axe, and Lady Myrtle Jellicoe (1908-45, later Lady Myrtle Balfour).

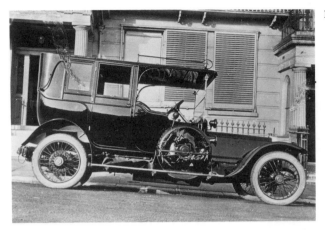

113. 45 hp Daimler belonging to the 2nd Sir Charles Cayzer (1869-1917) outside his house, 22 Lewes Crescent, Brighton 1909. The motor car significantly transformed the face of Perthshire and the way of life of its people. The motor car became the status symbol of the rich during 1895-1910, and by 1914 there were a third of a million cars on the roads of Britain. Many people favoured the Daimler, as Britain's first royal motorist, Edward VII, was driven for the first time in 1896 by the Hon. Evelyn Ellis in a Cannstatt-Daimler, thus starting an association between the Royal Family and the Daimler Company. Edward's first royal car was a 6 hp Daimler Model A.

114. The 3rd Sir Charles Cayzer (1896-1940) when a young man, on his Clymo motorcycle, outside Kinpurnie Castle in 1910. He was trained for the army and was a Member of the King's Bodyguard for Scotland (Royal Company of Archers), and served as Conservative M.P. for Chester from 1922 to his death. The first entirely British motorcycle was the 3 hp Holden, 1898. Registration plates were introduced in 1903.

115. Early Clymo motorcycle and sidecar belonging to the 3rd Sir Charles Cayzer. At the turn of the century the speed limit for all self-propelled vehicles was twelve miles per hour.

117. Captain Jack Murray RN at Strathallan, circa 1843.
Captain Murray lived at Croftinloan, some ten miles from
Dunkeld. He was in Queen Victoria's entourage during her
visits to Scotland in 1842 and the Blair Atholl visit of
1844.

116. The Hon. W.H. Drummond who later became 9th Viscount
Strathallan, at North Mains. He was born in 1810 and was
Lord-in-Waiting to Queen Victoria 1858-9, 1866-68. He
died in 1886, and was a pioneer photographer, this is a self-
portrait.

THE DRUMMONDS OF MEGGINCH CASTLE

Megginch Castle lies within the parish of Errol in the Carse of Gowrie, eastern Perthshire. The structure dates in its oldest part from 1460 and has been the seat of the Drummond family since 1664. The castle was enlarged in 1820 by Captain (later Admiral) Adam Drummond, who also laid out the flower gardens. John Murray Drummond and his wife Frances added many plants and shrubs to the policies after 1840. Topiary work was carried out at Megginch to commemorate Queen Victoria's Golden Jubilee in 1887. In 1902 Captain Malcolm Drummond erected a sundial in the garden to celebrate the Coronation of Edward VII.

118. The Stable Yard, Megginch Castle, in 1876. Left to right the figures are: Mary Drummond (1852-1934) on 'Lady Glendower', Mrs J.M. Drummond of Megginch, with the butler's son, Ronald Stuart.

119. Megginch Castle, 1903, with the family Panhard. Left to right the figures are: the Hon. Mrs Geraldine Drummond and her kilted husband Malcolm Drummond, and chauffeur. In the car (front) are John Drummond (aged 3) and his sister Frances (6), (back seat) Jean Drummond (12) and Victoria Drummond (9). The family is assembled outside the 1820 entrance to the castle; a new front door, set within a circular tower, was constructed in 1928.

120. Miss Jean Drummond of Megginch (1891-1974), daughter of Malcolm Drummond of Megginch and Kilspindie, in her perambulator outside Megginch Castle. In later life she was involved in the organisation of the Queen Victoria Girl's Club, Lambeth. The first mention of baby carriages in Britain is the 18th century, but it was not until the first half of the 19th century that their use began to be widespread.

CHAPTER TEN
AND TELL OF THE TOWERS THEREOF

121. St Leonard's Free Church, King's Place, Perth, photographed by Alexander Wilson, 20 August 1892. The church stands at the South Inch and dates from 1882. The original church dates from 1843.

122. Perth Bridge leading across the Tay to Charlotte St and Tay St. The facade of the Art Gallery and Museum are clearly seen to the right as well as the Royal and British Linen Banks. Tay St was built 1870-75. The trees in Tay St were planted by Lord Provost Kirkwood, 1881-82. The harbour was built on what was called Sand Island after the railway bridge across the Tay prevented shipping from reaching the shore at Tay St.

123. Perth High St looking west towards St Paul's Church and the Glassite Meeting House. Glassites were the followers of John Glas who maintained that a congregation with its eldership, in its discipline, was subject to no jurisdiction but that of Jesus Christ; for that Glas fell foul of the Church of Scotland. In 1909 the Fair City Bar at 107 High St was managed by James Brow.

124. Anne, Duchess of Atholl and friends sketching in the ruins of Dunkeld Cathedral. The 14th century tower rises to the left and the great west door, centre, leads into the nave and is of 15th century date. Many relics of the Atholl family are to be found in the cathedral which was finally restored in 1908. The Atholl mausoleum lies in the old Chapter House.

125. Dunning Church. Dedicated to St Serf, this Norman structure and tower form a distinctive landmark in the parish. Its minister 1848-60, was Paton James Gloag, Moderator of the General Assembly, 1889.

126. The parish church and Drummond St, Muthill. The greater part of the parish lay on the Drummond Castle estate of the Earl of Ancaster. The village was a favourite place of call for the itinerant tinkers. The little boy (Charlie Stewart) in the foreground sports his highland dress (Victorian version) which became popular from the 1870s. Circa 1901.

127. A meeting of the Perth Guild Court, circa 1866. As with most medieval cities Perth had its trade guilds and the Guildry Incorporation was established to protect and supervise local craftsmanship and commerce. In 1210 the Charter of William the Lion confirmed the authority of the burgesses of Perth to have a merchants' guild.

128. Construction of Comrie Bridge over the River Lyon, 1896, four miles west of Aberfeldy near Coshieville and Keltneyburn. Perthshire is a county of bridges and up to modern times many of the old masonry arch bridges built before 1830 were in use.

129. During 1897 Queen Victoria celebrated her Diamond Jubilee. Most towns and villages in Perthshire organised special events set up by committees. On 22 January 1897 the Pitlochry Celebration Committee met to discuss their plans. From left to right are: S R Skinner, William Robertson, draper, William Martin, grocer, Lachie Mackay, newsagent, and, Henry Smith, baker.

130. The laying of the foundation stone of a boys' boarding-house, New Wing (later known as Skrine's) on 1 October 1891 by William Ewart Gladstone at Glenalmond College. The then Warden is on Gladstone's right and behind stands the Rev. Dr J.H. Skrine after whom the building was named. The New Wing was eventually opened for use in 1893. Of the party that day were the Marquess of Lothian, Bishop Wordsworth of St Andrews, Bishop Barry of Sydney, Australia and Bishop Browne of Winchester.

131. An election rally, Tay St, Perth. The posters refer to William Whitelaw who was Conservative MP for the City of Perth 1892-95, and who lived at Huntingtower House. Also mentioned is W.L. Boase who unsuccessfully contested the Eastern division of Perthshire for the Conservatives; he lost to the Home Rule Liberal, Sir John Smyth Kinloch, who served until 1903.

132. The opening of the Sandeman Library, Kinnoull St, Perth, 22 October 1898. The ceremony was conducted by the Rt Hon The Earl of Rosebery (he stands on the steps with an umbrella on his right arm). Rosebery had been Prime Minister in 1894. The library was the result of the bequest of Professor Archibald Sandeman of Queen's College, Cambridge.

133. King Edward VII lunched at Cromlix House in September 1908, after having opened the Queen Victoria School, Dunblane. He is bidden farewell in the photograph by his host Col Arthur William Hay Drummond (d. 1953). Col Hay Drummond of Cromlix served in the Berkshire Regiment and was the grandson of the Earl of Kinnoull. The Cromlix area was once the episcopal barony of the Bishops of Dunblane and passed to the Drummond Viscounts of Strathallan at the Reformation and later to the Drummond Hays, Earls of Kinnoull. Edward VII and Queen Alexandra travelled to Scotland to spend a month each summer at Balmoral. Many a Scottish laird updated his family home in the hopes that the King (he was Prince of Wales up to 1901) might call. Indeed a visit by Edward VII was a nerveracking affair; he usually travelled with a huge convoy which accommodated his enormous suite consisting of a valet to cope with some forty suits and uniforms and twenty pairs of boots and shoes necessary for a stay of more than a week, a sergeant footman, a brusher, two equerries who needed a valet apiece, two secretaries, two drivers and an Arab boy to prepare coffee the way Edward liked it. Should he wish to go shooting the King also had two loaders and one for each of his equerries. If his wife was with him she would have a staff of six including a hairdresser, ladies-in-waiting and personal servants.

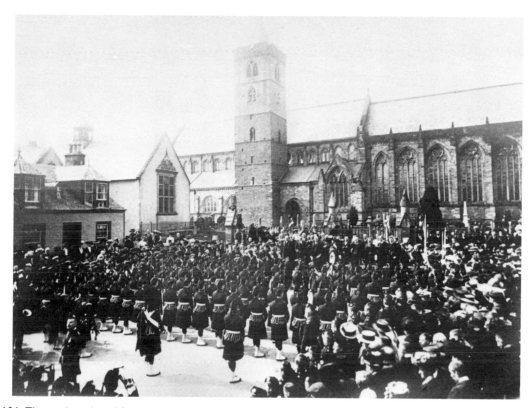

134. The proclamation of George V as King by Provost Murray Stewart of Dunblane. Provost Stewart is seen wearing the uniform of a captain of the Black Watch, in Cathedral Square, May 1910. In the picture are contingents of the Scottish Horse and Black Watch Territorials. Also pictured is the Rev. Alexander Christie, minister of the cathedral from 1886-1917 . . . he first conceived the idea of restoring the medieval cathedral, and worked to see its fruition.

135. Crowds awaiting the arrival of King Edward at Coupar-Angus station; this is thought to be when the King came to Balmoral via Blairgowrie. Coupar-Angus was the junction on the main Perth-Aberdeen line; circa 1907.

136. Provost Kerr at the Murray Fountain, Crieff, reading the proclamation of the accession to the throne of George V, 11 May 1910. Kerr served on the local council from 1883 to Nov 1910 and was the first Crieff provost to make a royal proclamation.

137. The Earl of Ancaster of Drummond Castle drives with Crown Prince William past the Station Hotel, Crieff, 1907. They were on their way to the Crieff Highland Games. William, Crown Prince of Germany and Prussia was the eldest son of William II, Emperor of Germany ('Kaiser Bill' of World War I).

138. Erected to the memory of the 6th Duke of Athole in 1866, the monument at Dunkeld is on the site of a much older cross. The monument contains drinking fountains, one for humans, with chained cups, and one for horses. On the monument is clearly seen the heraldic shield which linked the Dukes of Athole with their properties in the Isle of Man.

CHAPTER TWELVE
HOW WAGES WERE EARNED

BLACKSMITHS, firemen, butchers, gamekeepers are all seen as wage earners in this chapter, and indicate the diversity of employment available in Victorian and Edwardian Perthshire. Agriculture, forestry and allied jobs offered a rich employment but the average standard of living was low. A typical Perthshire urban family in the first few years of Edwardian Scotland would have had a weekly income of just £1.16.10d (£1.84) to look after a family of four children and two adults. They would have lived in a rented terrace house, have no transport of their own and found most entertainment at the local pub and within their own parlours. Almost two-thirds of their total income would go on food. In 1904 milk was 2d a pint compared with petrol at 1/7d a gallon and the average family consumed 10 pints of milk a week, 6½lbs of meat and 17lbs of potatoes. The living was hard compared with today.

139. David Greenhill, weaver, Abernethy. The loom was in Kirk Wynd. By 1900 few weavers worked at home.

140. Craftsmen abounded in Victorian Perthshire. Here a cobbler sits in his shop in Blairgowrie and earns a living from local footwear. Footwear fashions began to change with the coming of Queen Victoria. Riding boots for men gave way to shoes and women wore flat-heeled shoes with square-toes and satin shoes for evening. In the picture the cobbler is mending a 'tacketty' boot, the customary footwear for the workingman.

141. The heroes of every local urchin, the Perth fire brigade pose with their fire master. The formation of a City of Perth Fire Brigade was a consequence of meetings in 1835 to prepare a document on fire fighting in the city. It is reported that the new Brigade's first fire was at Fleming's Spinning Mill, Horse Cross. By 1850 a Central Fire Station was sited in Tay St. Fire Brigades were also operated from Perth Barracks and by Messrs J. Pullars & Sons from 1859.

142. Fishermen on the Tay below Abernethy. The third from the right is Andrew Scobie and the second from the right is George Scobie. Nets were stretched across the Tay to catch the salmon. The salmon were nearly all sent to Perth for the London market. The first experiments in the propagation of salmon by artificial means took place at Stormontfield in 1853.

143. Woodcutters in the hills above Abernethy. Wood was a very important commodity in Victorian Britain and fetched a high price amongst wood turners and furniture makers. Forestry in Perthshire has a long history; planting at Drummond Hill on the Breadalbane Estate commenced, for instance, in the 16th century.

144. Every community had its stane-knapper, the man who broke the stones for the road surface. Robbie Napier, the Comrie stane-knapper, had the additional advantage of possessing two thumbs. He would have had cartloads of quarried stone-tipped off at the road metal depot and he was paid so much a cubic yard to break down the stones to the size of a hen's egg. Robbie was a keen angler and skilfully made his own lines from horse-tail hair.

145. Maggie Clark, with tub and washboard, endeavours to shift the stubborn stains with elbow grease and Tay water, before the invention of biological powders. She stands at the 'Slappie' near Telford's bridge (1809) at Dunkeld.

146. Blairgowrie Smiddy at Upper Allan St, demolished in 1970. William Hally is on the left. The circle on the ground is for hooping wheels. The work of the blacksmith declined with the coming of the tractor and the resultant decline in the use of the horse.

147. Ruthvenside, or sometimes called 'The Baads', Auchterarder. The man with the beard is David Hally, his third son, John, is on the left. Young David sits on the plough; he eventually went to Canada. The men stand before an impressive display of ploughs.

148. In country districts a rabbit for the pot was an important part of domestic housekeeping and there was always someone willing to supply an illicit catch. Katie Swanson was a well-known poacher around Blairgowrie; she doubled up as the ferry crossing keeper. Her son was drowned in the record flood of 1913.

149. The station master, Crieff, 1896. Situated in the heart of Perthshire and on the fringe of the Highlands, Crieff was a popular health resort and holiday centre. The Crieff Junction (Gleneagles) Railroad of the Caledonian Railway Company was inaugurated in 1856; a direct link to Perth was opened in 1866 and to Comrie and beyond in 1893.

150. D. McGrouther's butchery delivery cart at the Black Watch Memorial, Aberfeldy. The memorial was unveiled the year of Queen Victoria's Jubilee, 1887, by Gavin, Marquis of Breadalbane, before an estimated crowd of 5000 people.

151. A Blairgowrie coalman. He sold single bags of coal to folk who could not afford bulk deliveries. In Perthshire coal was found on the Blairadam estates, a branch of the Kelty seams.

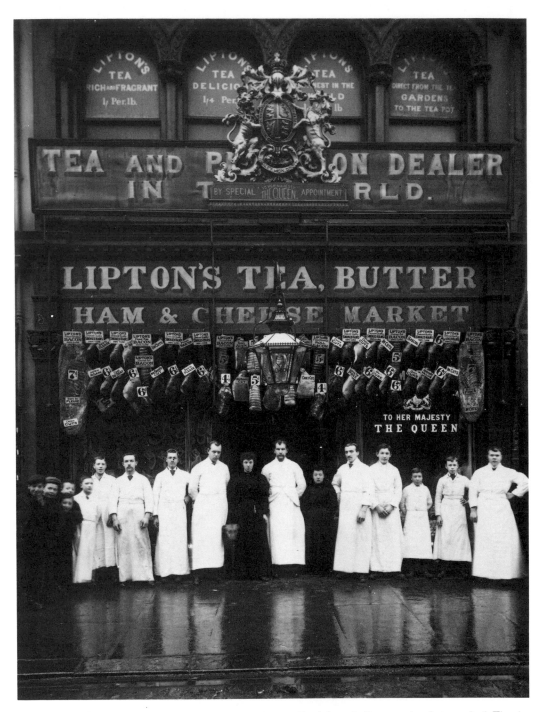

152. The staff of Thomas Lipton Tea and Provision Merchant, Perth branch, line up to be photographed. The shop proudly shows off its 'Special Appointment' to Queen Victoria warrant and the display records a fascinating set of prices. Grocers had to learn the arts of window adornment to tempt their customers. In the late 1890s Liptons were at 186 South St, and by 1910 they were at 32 South Methven St, Perth.

153. Perth slaughterhouse supplied employment of a distinctive nature to those who were not squeamish. Despite the introduction of refrigerated meats at lower prices, the housewife continued to prefer freshly killed meat if she could afford it. Even in the late Victorian times some 'slink' butchers sold meat from animals who had died of disease.

154. John Macgregor, butcher, Bank St, Aberfeldy. Meat consumption was always a sensitive indicator of living standards and specialist butchers' shops grew rapidly in Perthshire between 1880 and 1914.

155. Because of the attraction of the grouse moors for the gentry the number of gamekeepers in Scotland almost doubled betwee

156. Deerstalking was a popular pursuit amongst the gentry. This is the end of a day's stalking on the Atholl Estates, circa 1880.

6 and 1868. These are the hillmen and the gamekeepers of the Atholl estate in 1886 taken at Blair Castle. Regular photographs were taken of these men which reflected the esteem in which they and their work were held.

157. Three generations of Balquhidder weavers show the various stages through which wool undergoes the conversion from yarn to garment. In bygone days a housewife's first duty after marriage was to weave her own shroud and those of her family.

158. Jimmy Laurie, Dunkeld's bellman, prepares to announce a local event. Jimmy also was a school janitor and shoemaker. In 1515 the Chancellor of Dunkeld cathedral founded a school which was a forerunner of the Royal School.

159. Andrew Graham, van driver, for the Co-op at Crieff, circa 1910. In his hand he is holding the brushes with which he groomed his horse. Van drivers and delivery men were employed by every reputable business in Victorian and Edwardian Perthshire.

160. Lawman faces accused in this Victorian courtroom scene at Perth. The court clerks sit in front of the presiding lawyer while another reads the indictment. The law was administered through the JP Courts, the Circuit Courts of Judiciary, the Burgh and Guild Court, the Burgh Licensing Court and the Sheriff Courts at County Building, Tay Street.

161. Charles Fox, chimneysweep. The picture is taken along the characteristic walling of Taymouth Castle, about two miles from Kenmore on the road to Aberfeldy. Coal-fires demanded regular chimney sweeping and provided a steady job and income for local sweeps.

162. Young's Posting Station, Speygate, Perth, 1898. The adverts are hardly recognisable today. Advertising developed as the multiple stores like Liptons and the Maypole vied with each other to promote a faster turnover.

164. Ginger Harris delivered rolls for Andrew Jack, the Dunkeld baker. In those days shops relied on a fleet of delivery boys and some shops stayed open until 10 pm.

163. Postman John Lamb, delivering mail to Dungarthill Estate. We are told by Rev. Tom Dick that Lamb's grandson, Ian Lamb, still takes his turn at the round.

165. Blacksmiths at Pollythack Smiddy, Muthill. While the horse remained the essential means of transport, the blacksmith was a key village craftsman. His forge offered a diversity of manufacture from horse-shoes to the making of agricultural implements. The blacksmiths in the picture John Taylor (r) and Lachie Tavish (l) were also wheelwrights. Circa 1900.

166. James Deuchars of Blairgowrie had one of the first steam driven carting lorries; he acted as a coal merchant and moved heavy loads. This Foden had a speed of 5 mph; the Foden Company had introduced the '5 tonners' in 1902.

167. The Boys' Brigade, Muthill School outside the parish church, circa 1910. They pose with Major Wilkie their instructor. The Boys' Brigade had been founded in 1883 by William Alexander Smith at Glasgow.

168. A berrypicking scene at Essendy, Lethendy parish, circa 1910. Perthshire's raspberry harvest called for a large number of casual workers and the season lasted from 4 to 6 weeks. William McIntyre of Essendy employed schoolgirl labour and had dormitories equipped with adequate cooking facilities to house them. The boom in raspberry growing—usually a small holding activity—was at its height in 1901 and the bulk of the fruit went for jams and jellies.

169. The 'Quality Control Laboratory' of the local brewery in Allan St, Blairgowrie, 1900.

170. Owned by George Goble (fifth from the left), Birnham Smiddy was the home of the coachbuilders Goble and Loutit. The boy on the left holds a fore-hammer and his brother, second on the right, a draw plane. The implement held second left is a variable angle for checking curvatures of wheels. It is thought that the mechanism in the centre might be for testing brakes. The picture dates from 1866. Blacksmith's shops often descended from father to son through several generations. Apprentices were easily come-by in the harsh economic climate of Victorian Perthshire.

171. The hotel staff of the Stirling Arms, 1876. Servants wages were around £12 per annum. Hours of work were 6am to 6pm, six days a week. Three days holiday were allowed every year. Robert Burns stayed at the hotel in 1787.

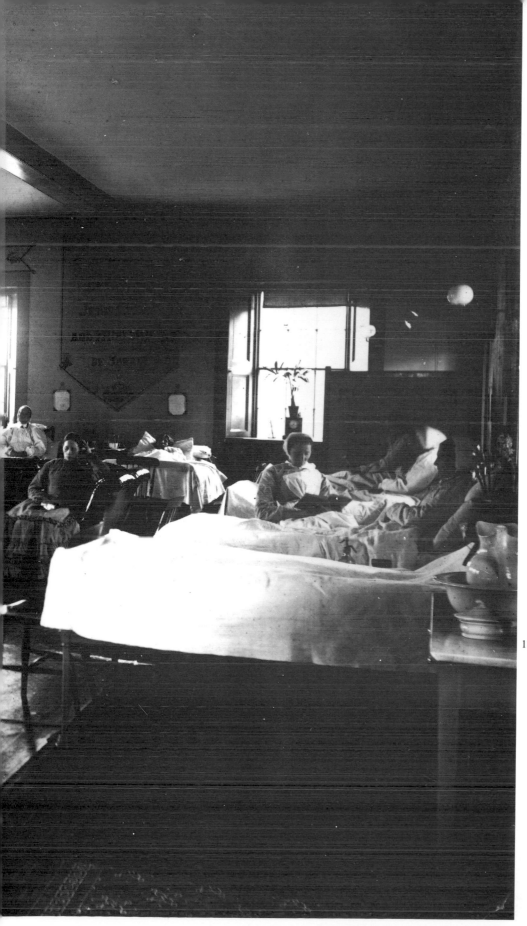

172. The female ward, Perth Hospital. The first infirmary at Perth was built in York Place 1837-38 and remained in use as a hospital until the Royal Infirmary was opened in 1914. The decor of the ward is redolent of the sickening Victorian cant which surrounded the poor and ill.

173. Victorian portraiture is a valuable record of life and activities of a vanished society. Prints which record the customs, work and work-costume of Victorians are quite rare. So this picture of a Perth basketseller is doubly interesting. With such pictures as this, photography became involved as a documentary medium and it gained recognition as an art form.